Elevate Your Mindset
Unlocking the Power of Beliefs

Edgar W. Kelly

Table of Contents

The mind is everything. What you think, you become.

— Buddha

Chapter 1. Introduction

Unleash a new version of yourself with our enlightening Special Report: "Elevate Your Mindset: Unlocking the Power of Beliefs!" This unique and insightful guide explores the compelling world of beliefs and mental frameworks, illuminating how they shape our lives every day. If you've ever felt trapped by your own thoughts or limited in your personal or professional progress, then this Special Report exists just for you. Dive in and discover how to master your mind, transform your beliefs, and catapult yourself towards your dreams. By the end, you'll not only feel enlightened but inspire yourself to embrace the endless possibilities life has to offer - all through the power of an elevated mindset. It's not magic, it's just mastery over your beliefs, and it's ready and waiting for you. Don't miss out on this exciting opportunity to ignite your potential and turn your life around!

Chapter 2. Understanding Mindsets: An Introduction

Every journey, every adventure, every revolution, they all commence with a single step. And so, we step into the great arena of mindsets with an understanding that our mental frameworks are essentially the architects of our own realities. They are the backstage managers, the invisible hands that are consistently and persistently shaping our experiences, perceptions, behaviors, and even our physical realities.

Particularly in the context of personal growth and development, the significance of cultivating the correct mindset cannot be overstressed. Picture yourself standing at the entrance to a labyrinth of your own mind, where every turn denotes new choices and decisions. Every step you take is guided by the mindset that you have nurtured and developed over the years. If your mindset is rigged with fear, doubt, and negativity, you find yourself increasingly gravitating towards this particular pattern. However, if your mindset is built on positivity, resilience, and an unwavering belief in possibilities, the road you take moves progressively towards these aspects.

2.1. In the Beginning Was the Mindset

But where do these mindsets come from? Mindsets can be traced back to our early years. It's during the initial stages of our lives that our minds begin to construct beliefs about the world, about people, about potential, about everything. These beliefs, these assumptive truths we tell ourselves, then serve as the foundational bedrock of our mindsets. Be it supportive or unsupportive, affirming or disaffirming, ambitious or defeatist, these mindsets find their existence in our initial interpretations and understandings of our own personal realities.

Even though these mindsets get tucked away deep into the crevices of our subconscious minds, they radiate an influence that seeps into our every thought, feeling, and action. Therefore, recognizing, understanding, and navigating these mindsets becomes an imperative for those seeking peak performance, achievement, and personal fulfillment.

2.2. The Anatomy of a Mindset

As we delve further into the structure of mindsets, we can conceptually divide a mindset into two main components: beliefs and attitudes. Beliefs refer to the assumed truths or realities that we have accepted about ourselves, others, and the world around us. These beliefs, which can either be limiting (such as "I am not smart enough") or empowering ("I am capable of great things"), lay down the foundations for our attitudes.

Attitudes, on the other hand, are the emotional and behavioral manifestations of our beliefs. They dictate our responses to life's varied instances, shaping our reactions, decisions, and actions. For example, if you hold the belief that failure is part of growth, your attitude towards setbacks would be one of learning and resilience.

2.3. From Fixed to Growth: The Dual Mindset

Renowned psychologist Carol Dweck introduced the concept of 'Growth and Fixed Mindsets." The Fixed Mindset refers to the idea that our intelligence, abilities, and qualities are static and unchangeable. The Growth Mindset, as a contrast, postulates that our abilities and intelligence can be developed and honed over time through experience, learning, and resilience. But it is not just about the possibility of growth; it is a belief that actively encourages it.

It is vital to note that these mindsets aren't just concepts or constructs. These are powerful belief systems influencing how individuals perceive their capabilities, confronting challenges, and setting the trajectory of their lives.

2.4. Mindsets Matter: The Power of Perspective

As we gradually cement our understanding of mindsets, the sheer power they possess becomes evident. They are not just about positive thinking or about having an optimistic outlook. They delve much deeper, permeating into our very identities, sculpting our personalities, our behaviors, and even our destinies. After all, the lenses through which we perceive the world have a profound impact on the world that we experience.

It might appear redundant to emphasize the significance of our mental dispositions, but their impact is so far-reaching that one cannot afford to neglect the power that mindsets hold. They are the silent puppeteers, potentially dictating every aspect of our existence – from how we think, feel, dream, and strive, to how we love, interact, learn, and even falter. They draft the vision board of our lives, and hence, understanding their profound implications is not just a choice, but a necessity for those who desire to chart the course of their lives.

In the chapters that follow, we will journey through the terrain of beliefs - their formation and function. We will uncover how we can address and unlock the limiting beliefs that may keep us entangled in negative thought patterns. We will explore the power and art of affirmations, the process of cognitive restructuring, and venture into goal setting, emotional intelligence, mindfulness, and the immense potential that visualization holds. The forthcoming chapters would help to comprehend how beliefs and mindsets interact and influence one another, while also equipping us with transformative tools to allow the evolution and growth of our mindsets.

In conclusion, establishing a robust and beneficial understanding of mindsets is the primary step in our ultimate quest to unlock the power of beliefs and their consequential progression into the reality of our individual lives. As we commence this journey, the understanding of our mindsets becomes an insightful starting point for our exploration into the realm of beliefs, their transformation, and the ensuing empowerment. Let this exploration be a liberating one, unlocking doors and breaking barriers, not just in our minds but also in the broader expanse of our lives.

Chapter 3. The Foundation of Beliefs

As we embark on this intellectual journey, it is vital to understand where beliefs stem from and how they form the bedrock of how we perceive ourselves and the world around us. Delving into the foundation of beliefs, we shall shine light on what beliefs are and how profoundly they shape our thoughts, actions, behaviour, and the very fabric of our existence. We will venture into psychological perspectives, development, types of beliefs, and their evolutionary grounds to cogently establish their cardinal role in our lives.

3.1. The Psychological Perspective

Belief formation roots itself deeply in psychology. Primarily, cognitive psychologists view beliefs as representations of knowledge that are formed through the process of thinking or cognition. A belief stems from perception, memory, consciousness, or even a combination thereof. Each belief is a mental construct, a conclusion we derive based on the subjective interpretation of our experiences. For instance, if a child touches a hot surface and gets burned, they form the belief that 'hot surfaces cause pain,' thus avoiding such surfaces in the future. So, our experiences and perceptions inject substance into our beliefs and structure our mental models of the world.

3.2. The Development of Beliefs

Beliefs do not blossom overnight, but rather they develop and evolve over time. This development is heavily influenced by genetic predisposition, childhood experiences, cultural background, social interactions, and personal experiences. The beliefs formed during childhood are potent, often becoming engrained due to the impressionable nature of a child's mind. For example, if a child grows up listening to stories of remarkable human feats, they might grow up believing in the power of human resilience and potential. These beliefs can be further reinforced by societal values, education, and experiences in later stages of life.

Cognitive dissonance theory suggests that we are naturally inclined towards reducing discrepancies between our beliefs and actions. If an individual discovers contradictions between their beliefs and reality, they attempt to either modify their beliefs or change their perception of reality. This cognitive adjustment process forms an essential part of the growth and evolution of our beliefs.

3.3. Types of Beliefs

Generally, beliefs can be categorized into two types – descriptive and normative. Descriptive beliefs, also known as 'is beliefs,' are our perceptions about what is factual and true in the world. They are our understanding of how the universe operates. On the other hand, normative beliefs, also termed as 'ought-to-be beliefs,' relate to morality, dictating what is right and wrong, good and bad. These are our moral compass guiding us through the labyrinth of life choices.

Each category affects our lives in distinct ways. Descriptive beliefs shape our understanding and interpretation of the world. They govern our thoughts, ideas, and perceptions about the physical and metaphysical world. Whereas normative beliefs shape our values, ethics and principles, governing our actions and responses towards various life situations.

3.4. The Evolutionary Grounds of Beliefs

Evolutionary psychology contributes a unique perspective to belief formation. Human beliefs often accompany a survival advantage or reproductive benefit. For instance, early humans who believed that 'fire is dangerous and can cause death' were more likely to survive, passing down this belief and their genes to future generations. Similarly, social beliefs in cooperation and altruism that emerged in early human societies had survival benefits, leading to their preservation across generations. The fear of unseen forces, leading to the formation of belief in gods and deities, probably stemmed from our need for structure and predictability in a chaotic world.

Beliefs have been a cornerstone of human existence and evolution. They're central to how each one of us perceives, interprets, and interacts with the world. Understanding the foundation of beliefs would be incomplete without stressing the fact that while some beliefs help us grow and prosper, others can limit our horizons and hinder personal growth. It is, therefore, important to evaluate our beliefs time and again, ensuring they empower rather than confine us in our personal and professional endeavours. This evaluation is a step towards acquiring command over our beliefs, setting us on course to master the power of an elevated mindset.

While that's the encompassing ground of the chapter, do keep in mind that the cornerstones laid down remain raw without continual inspection and reinforcement as our beliefs shape us, guide us, and sometimes restrain us. It is through their understanding and manipulation that we can truly unlock potentials hitherto unknown to us. The following chapters would delve into decoding negative belief patterns which often act as hurdles, and then introducing positive reinforcements through affirmations and cognitive restructuring. Through this, we aim to guide you towards adopting a progressive and growth-oriented belief system. Get ready to welcome an enlightened 'You'.

Chapter 4. Decoding Negative Self-Belief Patterns

Within the realms of our mind lie a puzzling maze of beliefs - positive, neutral, and negative. Far too often, we find ourselves succumbing to the sinister grip of negative self-belief patterns. Considered a major impediment to personal growth, these patterns can stifle potential, undermine confidence, and hinder progress. In this engaging narrative, we endeavor to unravel the intricacies of negative self-beliefs. We shall dissect their origins, understand their impact, and finally, offer strategies to escape their clutches.

4.1. Origin of Negative Self-Belief Patterns

Negative self-belief patterns, much like their positive counterparts, have their genesis in a repertoire of past experiences. These experiences, primarily from childhood and adolescence, quietly sculpt our underlying cognitive frameworks about ourselves and our capabilities. Family background, societal conditioning, traumatic incidents, or recurrent failures often serve as the founding bedrock of these self-defeating belief systems.

Inculcated at an impressionable age or during vulnerable phases, these beliefs dig their roots deep within our psyche, presenting themselves as the 'undeniable truth' about ourselves. We might, over time, accept them as an intrinsic part of our identity; a 'reality' we must contend with. But in truth, they are mere distortions, crafted by our minds under the influence of past events, bereft of any empirical validity in the present or future.

4.2. Impact of Negative Self-Belief Patterns

The domino effect of negative self-belief patterns affects every sphere of our lives - interpersonal relationships, career growth, emotional wellbeing, and overall quality of life. Their imprint can be witnessed in our behaviors, emotions, and thought processes.

Self-limiting beliefs tend to predispose us towards a pessimistic interpretation of life events, often leading to a self-fulfilling prophecy. For instance, the belief "I am bad at networking" might discourage an individual from initiating conversations at social events, thereby reinforcing their initial assertion.

Such patterns can engender feelings of low self-esteem, unhappiness, and even lead to mental health issues such as anxiety, depression, and a general feeling of discontent. The vicious cycle, thus formed, can be significantly detrimental to both our psychological wellbeing and our quest for personal achievement.

4.3. Strategies to Decode and Disrupt Negative Self-Beliefs

The journey from ingrained negative self-beliefs to a liberated mindset begins with decoding these patterns and then disrupting their continuity. This process can be achieved through self-reflection, cognitive restructuring, and cultivating a growth mindset.

Self-reflection is the mirror to our soul's internal workings. Investing time and patience to dissect our thought patterns, identity recurring negative beliefs, and understanding their context is paramount to their deconstruction.

Cognitive restructuring, a buzzing term in the field of psychology, refers to the process of challenging and changing maladaptive beliefs. Its techniques include analyzing the evidence supporting our beliefs, reframing our thoughts and assumptions, and consciously choosing to replace self-defeating thoughts with positive affirmations.

A **growth mindset** embodies an understanding and acceptance that abilities and intelligence can be developed. Cultivating such a mindset can serve as a sturdy shield against these destructive beliefs, fostering resilience and promoting self-development.

Through a blend of these strategies, breaking free from the chains of negative self-belief patterns is indeed achievable.

Decoding negative self-belief patterns may seem a daunting task, requiring considerable effort and perseverance. However, the rewards it offers in terms of personal freedom, self-acceptance and unlocking potential are unparalleled. Equipped with a deeper understanding of negative beliefs and a toolset to disentangle them, we are on an invigorating path to reclaim the reins of our mind.

Remember that these beliefs are not the yardstick by which we must measure ourselves. The 'truth' they present is merely a distorted reflection, a fallacy drummed up by past experiences and fears. As we continue our journey, let's strengthen our resolve to dismantle these harmful constructs and unlock our fullest potential, all the while striving towards an elevated mindset that empowers and uplifts.

Chapter 5. The Science of Self-Talk: Crafting Positive Affirmations

Self-talk, in its essence, refers to the constant stream of thoughts that run through your mind every day. These thoughts can either be conscious or unconscious, with many occurring even without our immediate awareness. While self-talk is often dismissed as insignificant background chatter, its influence over our thoughts, emotions, and behaviors is profound.

5.1. Unravelling the Complexity of Self-Talk

Before delving into the art of crafting positive affirmations, it's crucial to understand the science behind self-talk. It might seem like an innate, uncontrollable stream of thoughts, but multiple factors influence its nature and effects.

Psychologists have long studied self-talk as an essential aspect of cognition and its undeniable impact on emotional health and productivity. The way you converse with yourself influences not only your perceptions about the world but also your reactions and choices. Your self-talk forms the foundation of the worldview you possess, directly impacting your belief system and, consequently, your actions.

Whether or not you acknowledge it, self-talk plays an influential role in shaping your reality. So prevalent is this internal conversation that it's been documented to occur at the rate of between 300 to 1,000 words per minute. This continuous dialogue can be both nurturing and destructive, depending upon its content and tone.

5.2. Distinguishing between Positive and Negative Self-Talk

Negative self-talk is often filled with self-criticism, self-doubt, and self-depreciation, which can lead to decreased self-esteem, heightened stress levels, and diminished motivation and performance. On the contrary, positive self-talk encourages self-validation, self-confidence, and self-appreciation, enhancing self-esteem and overall life satisfaction.

Indeed, positive and negative self-talk can be seen as two sides of the same coin; each influencing our self-concept, life outlook, emotional state, and behavioral patterns significantly. The key lies in acknowledging this and consciously pivoting towards more positive, empowering self-dialogue.

5.3. The Principles of Positive Affirmations

Positive affirmations are constructive self-statements that we consciously choose to focus on. They encourage optimism, self-belief, and resilience, thus forming a critical tool for transforming negative self-talk into positive, empowering language.

Let's focus on various facets of positive affirmations:

- Intention - Affirmations should be intentional, with a clear and concise suggestion or command for the subconscious mind to comply with.

- Present tense - Positive affirmations should always be stated in the present tense, such as "I am," instead of projections onto the future like, "I will be."

- Personal - Affirmations need to be relevant to the individual using them, with personal relevance ensuring maximum emotional impact and effectiveness.

- Positive language - They should be framed in positive terms rather than focusing on eliminating negative traits. Instead of stating, "I am not stressed," a more positive framing would be, "I feel calm and relaxed."

- Repeated over time - The more often you repeat your positive affirmations, the more they'll get engrained into your subconscious mind, gradually transforming your thoughts, feelings, reactions, and behaviors.

5.4. Crafting Positive Affirmations: A Step-by-Step Guide

The process of creating potent positive affirmations begins with understanding the specific areas in your life where you wish to manifest improvement or change. Here are a detailed, comprehensive set of steps to aid you in creating powerful affirmations:

1. Identify your negative self-talk, beliefs, or behaviors - This might seem uncomfortable, but becoming conscious of your self-defeating or limiting scripts can provide crucial insights into areas requiring positive change.

2. Determine the positive opposite - Once you've identified a negative belief or behavior, figure out its positive counterpart. For instance, if you frequently catch yourself thinking, "I'm a poor public speaker," the positive opposite might be, "I am a confident and compelling communicator."

3. Craft your positive affirmation - Start by framing it in the present tense, followed by positive and personal language. For example, "I am enjoying my developing communication skills as they enhance my professional influence."

4. Practice your affirmation - Revisit and repeat your affirmations regularly, ideally at a fixed, reserved time during your day. Repetition strengthens the neural pathways associated with them, facilitating their incorporation into your belief system.

5. Affirm with emotion - Feel the words of your affirmation and visualize the outcome. This emotional connection escalates your affirmation's effectiveness as it enforces cognitive and emotional alteration.

6. Stay patient and consistent - Transformation doesn't happen overnight. Stay committed to your affirmation and give it time to work on your subconscious mind, gradually aligning your thoughts, feelings, and behaviors with the new positive narrative.

5.5. Illuminate Your Life with the Power of Positive Affirmations

The power that self-talk, especially positive affirmations, holds in shaping our lives is enormous. It's not a magical quick-fix but a transformational tool that, when used with sincerity and persistence, can lead to profound effects on your beliefs, emotions, and actions.

Understanding the significance of positive self-talk and harnessing it through affirmations helps reshape mental scripts, reconcile cognitive dissonance, and foster a proactive attitude towards life. The deliberate practice of positive affirmations, armed with knowledge about their science, empowers you to navigate life's ups and downs creatively, confidently, and optimistically.

In the journey towards an elevated mindset, the science and art of crafting positive affirmations serve as an indispensable ally. Stay patient with your progress, remain consistent with your practice, and be ready to greet a brighter, optimistic, and empowered version of yourself.

Chapter 6. Principles of Cognitive Restructuring

Cognitive Restructuring is a well-established therapeutic practice, often used in Cognitive Behavioural Therapy (CBT), which works on the principle of altering maladaptive thought patterns that can contribute to emotional distress or dysfunctional behaviour. The primary aim of this exercise is to help individuals unlearn the habit of unreasonable thought and replace it with patterns that are more conducive to emotional well-being and growth. As we delve deep into the nuances and methodologies of cognitive restructuring, let's begin with examining its foundation and understand how it can help you achieve an elevated mindset.

6.1. Understanding the Core Concept of Cognitive Restructuring

The heart of cognitive restructuring lies in the recognition and alteration of faulty thought patterns. Thoughts influence our emotions and our reactions to certain situations. Therefore, it's crucial to understand that distorted, unrealistic, and irrational thought patterns can lead to magnified emotional responses such as fear, anxiety, anger, and depression. Cognitive restructuring, thus, presents a method to break down these patterns, challenge belief systems, and replace them with healthier alternatives.

This doesn't imply that the process encourages mere positive thinking. Instead, cognitive restructuring advocates for realistic, balanced, and rationale thinking. It works to eliminate cognitive distortions, which are biased perspectives we have on ourselves and the world around us. They are irrational thoughts and beliefs that we unknowingly reinforce over time that distort our perceptions of reality.

6.2. The Four-Step Process of Cognitive Restructuring

Cognitive restructuring is often applied through a four-step model, as originally formulated by psychologist Dr. Aaron T. Beck. Every step acts as a building block to the final process of reforming your cognitive structure. So let's delve into them one by one.

1. *Thought Identification:* Recognizing our thoughts, especially negative or maladaptive ones, is the first step towards restructuring them. This may require mindfulness exercises or maintaining a thought diary—listing out situations, emotional responses, and consequent actions, which help in deciphering common underlying negative thoughts or cognitive distortions.

2. *Thought Evaluation:* Once you've identified negative thought processes, the next step is to evaluate them critically. This involves questioning the evidence behind the thought, its usefulness, and its potential long-term implications. A helpful tool in this process is the ABC Model, which stands for Activating Event, Beliefs, and Consequences. Understanding this association can lighten the impact of certain situations by focusing on the beliefs around them.

3. *Thought Replacement:* The third step in the process, as the phrase suggests, is to replace negative thoughts with positive alternatives. The goal is not to convert a negative thought into an overly optimistic one, but to provide a balanced, rational, and truthful version of it. It helps in maintaining emotional equilibrium, even in unfavorable situations.

4. *Thought Testing:* Replacing thoughts is not enough. They must be tested in real-life scenarios to gauge the efficacy of our thought restructuring. This could be done through behavioural experiments or visualization techniques to consolidate new, healthier thought patterns.

6.3. Techniques for Effective Cognitive Restructuring

While the four-step process forms the basis of cognitive restructuring, it's also important to practice and develop a few techniques to reinforce the process effectively. These techniques can aid in reshaping your beliefs more positively and persistently.

- *Socratic Questioning:* Named after the classical Greek philosopher Socrates, it's a form of disciplined questioning to dismantle your irrational and negative beliefs. It helps to expose contradictions in your thought process, delivering clarity and perspective.

- *Mindfulness Meditation:* Mindfulness activities cultivate the practice of staying present. It familiarizes you with different types of thoughts and helps in distinguishing maladaptive thoughts from the adaptive ones.

- *Behavioural Experiments:* They include real-life exposure to feared situations. It's a method of facing your negative thoughts instead of avoiding them, which helps to test the validity of these thoughts against actual evidence.

- *Redefining Personal Rules and Assumptions:* Our beliefs often stem from certain personal rules and assumptions we hold. Redefining these can help you see situations from an entirely new perspective.

In conclusion, cognitive restructuring is a scientifically proven, time-tested technique used for breaking down and reassembling our belief structure. Though it may initially seem like an uphill task, with patience and practice, it can go a long way in combating cognitive distortions and fostering an elevated, empowered mindset. You're not destined to be captive to unhelpful, irrational thought patterns. It's in your power to modify your thoughts and, therefore, your feelings—leading to noteworthy changes in your actions and life outcomes. Remember, the journey of cognitive restructuring is not a quick fix, but faithful perseverance can indeed produce transformation.

Chapter 7. Goal Setting: The Power of A Positive Mindset

The journey towards the mastery of our beliefs and mindset truly begins when we start to explore our goals and aspirations. Throughout this chapter, we'll examine the immense power of a positive mindset in the process of goal setting. We'll delve into the importance of goal setting, the process of setting effective goals, the concept of the Growth Mindset, and how all these elements interrelate.

7.1. Understanding the Importance of Goal Setting

Goal setting is a powerful procedure for visualizing your ideal future, and for motivating yourself to transform this vision into reality. The process of setting goals helps you choose where you want to go in life. By knowing precisely what you want to achieve, you are better able to concentrate your resources on reaching those goals.

Goals create a bridge between today's reality and the future you envision. Setting them gives you long-term vision and short-term motivation. By setting sharp, clearly defined goals that are measurable and time-bound, you can measure and take pride in their achievement, which consequently boosts your self-confidence.

7.2. The Process of Effective Goal Setting

The process of effective goal setting often begins with the articulation of what you want to achieve. These ambitions and desires are later broken down into smaller, more manageable goals, which ensure that you are constantly making progress. The SMART (Specific, Measurable, Achievable, Relevant, and Time-bound) goal-setting model helps us define goals that are effective and action-oriented.

For each of your goals, take time to apply the SMART model:

- **Specific**: Your goal should be clear and specific, otherwise you won't be able to focus your efforts or feel truly motivated to achieve it.

- **Measurable**: It's important to have measurable goals so that you can track your progress and stay motivated.

- **Achievable**: Your goal also needs to be realistic and attainable to be successful. In other words, it should stretch your abilities but still remain possible.

- **Relevant**: This step is about ensuring that your goal matters to you, and that it also aligns with other relevant goals.

- **Time-bound**: Every goal needs a target date, so that you have a deadline to focus on and something to work towards.

Further, to ensure continuous progress and maintain momentum, check in regularly on your goals. By reviewing them, you're able to measure your progress, recalibrate if needed, and stay on track.

7.3. The Power of A Positive Mindset

A positive mindset is an imperative element in this discussion. A person with a positive mindset views challenges as opportunities for growth, stays focused during adversity, and believes that they can overcome difficulties. This perspective enhances their abilities, amplifies their motivation, and ultimately leads to a higher likelihood of achieving their goals.

By believing in your ability to succeed, you'll be more likely to put in the necessary effort, become more resilient in the face of obstacles, and less likely to be discouraged by difficulties. All of this can contribute significantly to achieving your chosen goals.

7.4. Embracing the Growth Mindset in Goal Setting

The Growth Mindset, a concept introduced by psychologist Carol Dweck, is the belief that our abilities and intelligence can be developed with time, practice, and effort. It contrasts with a fixed mindset, the idea that our intelligence and capabilities are innate and unchangeable.

Embracing a Growth Mindset in the process of setting and achieving goals is transformative. It fosters resilience, encourages perseverance, and makes us more likely to overcome challenges, all hallmarks of successful goal achievement. When you believe you can grow, improve, and learn, you are more likely to work hard, apply necessary efforts, and persist in the face of difficulties.

7.5. Moving Forward with A Positive Mindset

As we surge ahead in our journey, engraving a positive mindset and using it as a guiding light while charting our growth path is paramount. Our mindset forms the foundation of our thoughts, feelings, and behaviors. Shaping it positively can have a domino effect on various aspects of our personal and professional lives, not just goal setting.

Embrace the process of setting, reassessing, and refining your goals. Nurture a positive and growth-oriented mindset. Recognize that failure is only a stepping stone to learning and growing, and not the end of the road. Each step you take brings you closer to your objectives. The only way of failing is in abandoning your dreams and goals due to hurdles. Continue to set your sights higher, cultivate a positive mindset, and watch as you unlock the unlimited potential within you.

By the time you reach the end of this odyssey, you'll see how a positive mindset is not just an accessory, but a game-changer in your goal-setting journey, powering your aspirations and catapulting you towards your dreams.

Chapter 8. The Art of Visualization: Seeing Your Way to Success

The art of visualization is an easy concept to understand, but it demands practice and fine-tuning to effectively harness its power. As humans, we possess an incredibly potent tool - our mind. The ability to form images, ideas, and sensations in our minds without any immediate input from the senses is a cognitive process called visualization. This chapter aims to unravel the immense potential of visualization, present its scientific basis, demonstrate how it can be incorporated into our everyday lives, and how it can catalyze our journey to success.

8.1. Understanding Visualization

Visualization is, essentially, the act of creating a mental image of a future event or outcome. It's a simulation your brain performs to prepare for possible scenarios. This cognitive process is ubiquitous in our daily lives and most of the time we deploy it unwittingly. Whether you're daydreaming about an upcoming vacation or mentally rehearsing a conversation you anticipate having, you're using visualization.

The power of visualization lies in the fact that our brains make very little distinction between an event we vividly imagine and an event we physically experience. Visualization incorporates not just picturing an event or outcome, but involves experiencing it with all senses.

8.2. The Science Behind Visualization

Neuroscience provides the machinery of proof that explains why visualization can be such an effective practice. In a study on brain patterns led by Dr. Guang Yue, an Exercise Psychologist at the Cleveland Clinic Foundation, it was found that a mere mental rehearsal of an action uses the same motor and sensory regions of the brain as the physical performance of that action. This demonstrates that the brain cannot differentiate well between a vividly imagined experience and a real one.

When you vividly visualize a particular act, your brain generates an impulse that tells your neurons to "perform" the movement. This creates a new neural pathway, a sequence of neurons that carry out a particular function, which primes your body to act in a way consistent with what you imagined. Consistent visualization can eventually lead to physical changes in muscle structure.

These scientific discoveries about "mental practice" have significant implications, especially for setting and achieving goals.

8.3. Principles of Effective Visualization

To leverage the power of visualization, it's not enough to just daydream. The effectiveness of visualization as a tool for success revolves around certain principles that need to be incorporated into the process.

Concreteness - The more detailed your visualization, the more effective it will be. Try to employ all your senses. What can you see? What can you hear? What can you feel or smell?

Frequency - The more often you visualize your success, the stronger and more resilient become the neural pathways that your brain forms. Prior research links frequency of mental rehearsal with improved performance of the visualized task.

Positive emotion - Emotion supercharges visualization. It's important to not just imagine the success, but also to feel the joy, the happiness, or the satisfaction that comes along with achieving your goal.

Consistency - It is important to visualize the same scenario or event in the same way each time, at least until it manifests into reality.

8.4. Incorporating Visualization into Daily Life

It's all well and good to understand the principles of effective visualization, but how do you put it to practice in your daily life?

Visualization fits easily into a daily routine. You can incorporate it during leisurely walks, break times, before you sleep, or even as a structured part of your morning routine.

Find a quiet place where you won't be interrupted, relax your body, close your eyes, and start building your desired reality in your mind. Incorporate the principles discussed - make your visualization lively and sensory filed. Feel the emotion deeply, repeat often, and maintain consistency in your visualization.

8.5. The Power of Visualization: From Thoughts to Reality

The power that visualization holds in pushing us towards success lies in its capability of persuading the subconscious mind. The deliberate imaginations we feed into our brain through visualization reshapes our self-image, unearths dormant capabilities, and propels us towards the realization of our goals. As Olympic gold medalist Michael Phelps's coach, Bob Bowman, puts it: "The brain cannot distinguish between something that's vividly imagined and something that is real."

Applying the art of visualization towards your personal, professional, or health goals, you provide a cognitive rehearsal for your brain and body, equipping you with the mental and physiological preparation that's needed to face real-life challenges. Your dreams don't have to stay within the confines of your thoughts. Instead, you can animate them into existence by constantly feeding your brain with successful outcomes and the emotions associated with them.

In conclusion, the art of visualization is not just about seeing; it's about believing, and more importantly, about making it happen - a vital tool in navigating the journey towards success.

Chapter 9. Cultivating Emotional Intelligence for Mindset Growth

Cultivating emotional intelligence plays a pivotal role in mindset growth. Emotional intelligence, or EQ, relates to our ability to recognize, use, understand, and manage our own emotions, as well as those of others. These abilities go far beyond the restrictions of a standardized IQ test or academic prowess. They are critical tools that empower us to navigate human interaction smoothly, enhance our professional and personal relations, tackle adversities with grace, and fortify our belief system to employees a more positive outlook.

9.1. Understanding Emotional Intelligence

Emotional intelligence, as put forward by psychologists Peter Salovey and John Mayer, is defined as the ability to monitor one's own and other people's emotions, to distinguish between different emotions and label them appropriately, and to use emotional information to guide thinking and behavior. The concept was later popularized by Daniel Goleman in "Emotional Intelligence: Why It Can Matter More Than IQ."

These skills can be broken down into four distinct but interrelated components: self-awareness, self-management, social awareness, and relationship management. Cultivating these key abilities forms the crux of elevating your emotional intelligence, ultimately leading to positive mindset growth.

9.2. Self-Awareness

This refers to the understanding of your own emotions, their triggers, their manifestations, and their impact. When we are tuned into our feelings, we are better equipped to handle scenarios that trigger these emotions, thus maintaining a composed mindset under pressure. Enhancing self-awareness requires constant introspection and the honest acknowledgment of emotions, however uncomfortable they might make you feel.

9.3. Self-Management

After becoming aware of our emotions, it is vital to manage them effectively. This involves disciplining our reactions, preventing negative emotions from spiraling, applying emotional control in times of stress, and staying positive despite setbacks. Techniques such as deep-breathing exercises, meditation, progressive muscle relaxation, and cognitive behavioral therapy can help in improving emotional self-control.

9.4. Social Awareness

An emotionally intelligent individual doesn't just understand their own emotions, but also the emotions of others. This ability to empathize allows them to communicate effectively, anticipate and meet the needs of others, and elevate their social standing. It cultivates individuals who are not just self-aware, but also socially sensitive and aware.

9.5. Relationship Management

The final component of emotional intelligence involves using the awareness of your own and others' emotions to manage interactions successfully. This includes the ability to develop and maintain healthy relationships, manage conflicts effectively, inspire and influence people, and express oneself clearly. Solid communication and negotiation skills are key to this facet of emotional intelligence.

9.6. Building Emotional Intelligence for Mindset Growth

In order to develop emotional intelligence, a concerted effort to practice the aforementioned components is necessary. * Regularly engage in introspection and mindfulness exercises to enhance self-awareness. * Employ stress management techniques to improve control over your reactions. * Practice active listening and empathy to develop social awareness. * Leverage strong communication and negotiation skills to manage relationships effectively and positive assertiveness.

By maintaining a disciplined approach to building emotional intelligence, you can foster an environment of understanding and empathy, both for yourself and for others. This can significantly contribute to your mindset growth, moving you towards a more positive, resilient mental framework.

9.7. Conclusion

Emotional intelligence is not an inborn trait, but rather, it's a set of skills that can be learned and cultivated over time. By developing these skills, we can initiate transformative changes in our lives, reshaping our mindset from a negative, reactive outlook to a positive, proactive one. The importance of emotional intelligence in mindset growth, then, cannot be overstated. With the insights provided in this chapter, and the implementation of the techniques detailed above, you stand ready to embark on your journey toward a more emotionally intelligent and positive mindset. This can act as a strong cornerstone in changing your belief system and gearing towards success, making it an integral part of 'Elevating Your Mindset.'

Chapter 10. Mindfulness and Its Role in Shaping Beliefs

The concept of mindfulness, often associated with ancient practices and Eastern philosophies, has gained popularity in recent years due to its profound impact on mental well-being, productivity, and the ability to shape one's beliefs. As opposed to being an inflexible construct, our beliefs and the worldviews they form are dynamic—capable of change and development. This transformative power stems from our capacity to be mindful. However, before we delve into the influence of mindfulness on beliefs, it's essential to understand what it truly means.

10.1. Defining Mindfulness

Mindfulness refers to the keen awareness and recognition of one's thoughts, feelings, bodily sensations, and surroundings in the present moment. Without judgement or the intent to control, it's a state of being in touch with reality as it unfolds. The power of mindfulness lies in its potential to help us understand our perception that guides our beliefs and behaviors.

10.2. The Link between Mindfulness and Beliefs

Beliefs shape our lives in profound ways, influencing how we perceive ourselves, interpret our experiences, and engage with the world. Our origins, cultural influences, and personal experiences all contribute to forming our belief system. However, these beliefs are not set in stone and can undergo change. The tool that facilitates this shift is mindfulness. By focusing and being present in the immediate situation, mindfulness encourages open-mindedness and critical thinking, which are instrumental in challenging and reshaping our beliefs.

10.3. Mindfulness, Beliefs, and Cognitive Bias

Cognitive biases often shape our beliefs. These biases make us pay more attention to certain types of information while disregarding others, leading us to form skewed beliefs. Through the art of mindfulness, we can identify these biases. By accepting our thoughts and emotions without judgement or resistance, we create a space to critically observe how our thoughts are biased and how these biases contribute to our beliefs.

10.4. Practicing Mindfulness

Awareness is the fundamental base of mindfulness. It might seem simple, but the act of complete awareness can be complex due to our constant exposure to stimuli and the inevitability of distractions. Mindful exercises like focused breathing, body scan, mindful listening, and mindful eating can help us cultivate this keen sense of awareness. Over time, these exercises familiarize us with identifying our thoughts, emotions, and biases in real-time, allowing us to understand their interplay in shaping our beliefs.

10.5. Mindfulness and Belief Transformation

The true power of mindfulness comes to the forefront when it is applied to transform our belief system. In the context of beliefs, mindfulness has two primary roles—awareness of existing beliefs, and facilitation of new, empowering beliefs.

Mindfulness helps us identify our limiting beliefs by encouraging us to attentively observe our emotions, thoughts, and behaviors. By gaining insight into how our beliefs are limiting us, we open the door to belief transformation.

In facilitating new beliefs, mindfulness fosters an environment of acceptance, openness, and non-judgment. This environment provides the fertile ground needed for the roots of new, empowering beliefs to take hold.

10.6. Integrating Mindfulness in Everyday Life

The key to leveraging mindfulness in belief transformation is integrating it into everyday life. Mindful moments can be incorporated everywhere, from eating meals and walking to work, to mundane tasks like washing dishes. The objective is to shift from being mindlessly automated to being attentively present.

10.7. The Journey of Mindful Belief Transformation

It is important to remember that mindfulness is not an instant solution; it is a journey. The process of belief transformation begins with understanding and accepting our current beliefs, continues with being mindfully aware of their impact on our lives, and culminates in the deliberate cultivation of empowering beliefs.

In conclusion, mindfulness is not just a state of awareness; it's a tool of transformation. By practicing mindfulness, we can impact our current belief system, replace limiting beliefs with empowering ones, and acquire the mindset necessary for personal growth and the achievement of our goals. Whether it's improving self-esteem, fostering a growth mindset, enhancing relationships, or overcoming fears, the power of mindfulness in shaping and remolding our beliefs is profound. Embrace the journey of mindfulness and unleash the power within!

Chapter 11. Case Studies: Success Stories of Mindset Shifts

This chapter ventures into real-life success stories that underscore the paradigm-altering power of mindset shifts. The lives, stories, and accounts shared in this section may seem far distanced from your life, but upon deeper reflection, you'll find them echoed across various aspects of your existence. You'll uncover that successful mindset shifts aren't confined within the realms of high achievement - they touch everything from the way we approach basic tasks to our interpersonal relationships and self-concept.

11.1. The Unwavering Athlete

Our first story throws the spotlight on an elite athlete named Sam, who was a long-jumper. Despite his natural talent for the sport and relentless training, he consistently found himself falling short of his potential during competitive meets. His physical abilities seemingly were unparalleled, yet his overall performance was inconsistent at best.

After a grueling series of disappointing performances, Sam sought the guidance of a mindset coach. His exploration into his mindset unveiled a deeply-seated belief that he was only as good as his last jump. This notion was shrouded in fear and continually drained his confidence.

Initially, Sam worked on reprogramming his internal narrative, replacing his self-deprecating beliefs with positive affirmations. He kept reminding himself: "I am a capable, successful athlete. One jump does not define me." Soon, he embraced visualization exercises, picturing himself executing perfect leaps.

The massive shift in his mindset did not translate into success overnight. It required persistent effort, patience, and consistency. However, over time, Sam's performances drastically improved. His confidence restored, he was able to outperform even himself, repeatedly breaking his personal records. He showed the world that shifting your mindset could indeed catapult you towards heights you've only dreamt of.

11.2. The Turnaround Entrepreneur

Our next case study revolves around Emily, a budding entrepreneur experiencing significant setbacks in her business. Despite having a promising business model and product, her venture remained stagnant. On analyzing her situation, Emily realized that her self-limiting beliefs were often presenting obstacles to progress. She held a firm belief that her lack of business education was entirely responsible for her shortcomings.

With the help of a business coach focusing on mindset shifts, Emily began to challenge her existing belief system. She engaged in cognitive restructuring and allowed herself to see the situation from a more positive perspective. Instead of considering her lack of a business degree as her downfall, she started recognizing it as a unique strength that allowed her to approach business un traditionally.

Emily also started practicing mindfulness. This helped her remain focused on the present moment, reducing the fear of future failures. She set SMART (Specific, Measurable, Achievable, Realistic, and Timely) goals that kept her focused on actionable steps rather than dwelling on her deficits.

The result was transformative. Emily's business experienced an unprecedented boost, and she began expanding her product line, catering to new markets, and strengthening her global presence. It was no miracle; it was merely the transformative power of shifting beliefs and adopting a robust, positive mindset.

11.3. The Fearless Public Speaker

Our final case study tells a tale of Steven, a gifted writer feared by the prospect of public speaking. Despite his enthralling storytelling ability, Steven was crippled by stage fright, which hindered him from sharing his literary work with wider audiences.

Recognizing the need for a mindset shift, Steven sought assistance from a communication coach. Together, they worked on modifying his terrifying belief that an audience would always be critical and dismissive.

Slowly, Steven started practicing cognitive restructuring techniques. He replaced the idea of an 'unforgiving audience' with 'an audience eager to listen and connect.' He also began using positive affirmations, reminding himself, "My words are powerful, and the audience will engage with my stories."

Steven decided to couple his newfound positive mindset with visualization techniques. He visualized himself standing on stage, captivating his audience, and receiving a standing ovation. He started practicing mindfulness, focusing on his breath during public speaking, which helped minimize his anxiety.

The once terrified storyteller transformed into a galvanizing public speaker. Steven's story showcases the incredible power of a mindset shift, ultimately leading to personal growth and unearthing untapped potential.

In conclusion, these stories serve as concrete evidence to the transformative powers imparted by mindset shifts. While every individual's journey is unique, the essence remains the same – replacing limiting beliefs with empowering ones to propel oneself into unchartered territories of success and self-growth. These life-altering experiences remind us of the beauty ingrained in embracing cognitive restructuring, positivity, visualization, and mindfulness as a holistic package impacting numerous life avenues. The next chapter we progress into shall continue the conversation on this transformatory journey, accentuating these collective experiences' lessons and their universal implications.

www.ingramcontent.com/pod-product-compliance
Lightning Source LLC
Chambersburg PA
CBHW070140230526
45472CB00004B/1621